Dedicated to all the women in my life
who have sustained my spirit, and still do...

Acknowledgements: *Absorb the Colors*, eds. Voldseth &
Herseth Wee, Heywood Press, 1984. A *Rich Salt Place*,
eds. Zelle, Easter, and Gery, Heywood Press, 1986.
Changeling, Coming Out, and Wonder (then called
Bone of Bone...), *Manitou Messenger*, St. Olaf College
newspaper, Northfield, MN, Mar. '91 & '92. *Before
Language*, Northfield Women Poets' Chapbook Series,
Heywood Press, 1992.

THE BOOK OF HEARTS

KAREN HERSETH WEE

THE
BOOK
OF
HEARTS

Merry Christmas,
Polly & Wil
with love —
Karen '93

THE BLACK HAT PRESS

ISBN 09614462-5-0

Manufactured in the United States of America

CONTENTS

Flying

Change

COMING OUT

BEFORE LANGUAGE

Daughter, sometimes I know your eyes follow
me and I would like to talk
to you in the language of women
easy in each other's company

So often when I try the words are wrong
My humor like a tune off-key
not well-received in your ear or your heart
But I promise I'll wait for a day

when we reach the same language
the sounds deep in our memories
of another time when in the womb
strumming the same chord we needed no words

CHANGELING

You arrived running
all bone & sinew
And on every photo after
one sock wrinkles down
Later word comes
from Lesbos
that you're here
only for a visit
I'd thought you mine
That I could own you
in my image
But you insist
and show me
that wonderful mind
of your own
revealing
the rib-locked secret
your becoming self
coming fast before
my very heart

ERMINE

A tall girl in large glasses perches
immobile on a log near a creek
Her rounded shoulders hunch against
                the nameless future   her lips move
but she makes no sound
            Her shadow steals away in the twilight

Nearby a small wary weasel stares out at her
        from beneath the roots of a fallen elm
                its head white against winter   body
        still soft brown   It watches the girl
while the creek flows   light fades   neither move
    When the snows come   it will have a new name

            She wonders   between the brown time
        and the white time, does an ermine
ever   not know   how to be   even with its friends
            Will she ever know
        the safety of a new season   a new name?

GENE

I don't remember
when I first knew
of the wild gene
loose in the family
But, dressed in fringed leather
I stalked it all my youth
from the back of a horse
and avoided men till one
unlike the others came
and stopped my quest
I saw it first though
in a farm-bred aunt
who left the farm by bus
to teach from coast to coast
Always on the move
she kept open invitation
wherever she lived
for those who didn't fit
Than a nephew drawn at ten
to the religion his mother left
to marry a Lutheran
sought a monastery education
like a moth finds flame
And you came
adept at math and music
and secrets   I am surprised
it took me so long
to recognize the gait
when at age one you careened
down the hall of our first home...
marked even then by the wild gene

WONDER

My mother and I wonder aloud to each other
My father and I -- loud wonders to each other
Sister and I wander away from each other
Brother and I, with little to wonder about...

Such a cushion to spring from -- more like
a trampoline -- all the tendons and bone
creating a springboard
and at any time any one of us
can fly out of sight
We keep doing our own individual leapings
our pirouettes, then springing off
one or the others' most recent event

Like last Easter in a brown S. Dakota park
The family was walking and talking
Two took strong issue
thought it the wrong time and place
but several others of us knew
it was just right for the announcement
made by a grandchild to her grandmother
about the grandchild's gayness
And she and the grandchild talked long
on a bench holding hands – the bone and sinew
keeping the tension just right between them
while others of us flew at each other
about timing and such, not admitting
the issue lay deeper than we could go
on a mere holiday. The real wonder was
the tendons, tissue and bone created a net
that held, even as some of us flew off and up
having a very long fall back

HOW TO SAY

I don't know how to say this:
You are not
what I expected
Your father and I came together
at a particular moment
in our knowing
and from deep inside me
you already were
made in the image
of the great god
who loves you even
more than I do

Made in my image too
of course, and your father's
those young years when you looked like him
the tomboy ones when
you walked like me
And now, a woman
on course
among careless teachings and wrong-
headed ones, you make your way
all the while reaching
a hand back to me
I will keep up, but am
not as young as you, nor as urgent
But I'm coming, dear heart
Don't get out of sight...
I *am* coming   and
                         I will bring others

THE READING

She comes late
sits at my feet
before the ten readers
and our audience
Come to hear
our instruments of voice
cadences of words
                    truth
hanging in the air
Her hand on my boot
is warm, she leans
this daughter heat
into my thigh
A summer child
sprung from my forehead
like Athena from Zeus
her baseball cap already
firmly on backwards
She sees
          differently
fundamental things
like music, math, love
possibility
the uncharted
routes of escape

BRINGING UP PARENTS

You, young parent in the city park
with your proud eyes following that child
over the jungle gym...
Think of it - she may be a baby dyke
the photos in her baby book
forever revealing
what you cannot yet name

Or you, with the brown-eyed son who loves
costumes   then lives in them
adopts another name for weeks at a time
insists on velvet, sometimes lace

Or the two of you, much decorated navy captain
and city librarian wife, with the ram-rod
young man taking all the honors in his class
at West Point, yet he seldom writes home
holds his secret so tightly to his chest
that if he held out his hands
he might fly straight off   the planet

So straight-
laced
this culture
narrow
no room
for a gay
heart
to spread
its wings
soar
Damage
done
early

Parents of gay children
throw off embarrassment   Send with pride
that family Christmas photograph with your daughter
holding her beloved's hand
New breed of pioneers
their child   much-loved grandbaby
cavorting between them
Two wonderful mommas
taking their urgent time
bringing us all up

GAY RESPONSE

The body and mind come together
at some galactic moment
out of time and space
and the givens of who
and what we are snap
to attention: our skin
color, eyes, our gender
sexuality comprise the whole--
but one thing missing:
How you respond to me
The first leg of my journey
the course I start on:
not mine to choose
That coursing of blood and bone
entwined in love or loss or hope
or hopelessness did that
But what turns there are
the forks, that's up to me: my choice
plus your response
Do not forget to take some
responsibility
I'll do what I can in the face
of that...

COMING OUT

All over town crab
apple trees have come out
blooming in the wrong season
the wrong climate
People have noticed
yet no one can account for it
so some have begun
to consult the specialists
Others hold that an early frost
last spring set the trees
on a different course
But in any event
it is nature, true nature
at her surprisingest
The way I see it
the only thing to do
is sit back, enjoy
or get out of the way
of their blooming
in our front yards
along roadways
and in the far distance
But I would urge you
to stop long enough to attend
closely their beauty
the fragileness of flower
Study the blooms & tight buds
the leaves coming out all around us
as most other midwestern trees turn gray

ORIGIN

OAHE

In Sioux
something firm to stand upon
earthen dams   human
or those in the mind
so much held back
How many years did it take
to have it feel good
to be home?

No apologies
I drown
in the warmth
it seeps under my skin
sustains
not quite
till next time
Oahe Dam
something firm to stand upon
Yet
it holds back
acres and acres   water
that weighs down bones
of sea creatures
buffalo   wolves
pioneers
a bleached mosaic tale
from before the days of salt
But what dam living
can hold back sorrow
acres and acres of tears
or   stem the flood of error?
Oahe
in Sioux
something firm to stand upon

GIVEN THREE SHELLS

Swirls, small creases, a crevasse
Brown trail arcing
around the gone snail
Like the trail we crawled slowly
in the heat last summer
up and around Bear Butte
in the Black Hills where prayer flags
waved, tipped with grain
placed carefully into the crooked
arms of old giant trees
And I remarked that it was wrong
I should be this old and know
about prayer flags in Nepal, in Japan
but *not* know of the Native American ones
fluttering in sacred trees
just fifty miles from home

GRANDMA BUNTROCK

O Tannenbaum, O Tannenbaum
we sang each Christmas Eve
at Grandma's house, Columbia, South Dakota
in the late thirties, early forties, the fifties
We stuffed fifty-three grandkids
moms and dads, aunts and uncles
into three skinny rooms.
None of us remember
Christmas eves in our own homes
We share one: same
house, decorated tree
carols, kaleidoscoped by time
through a hundred different pairs
of German hazel eyes

O Tannenbaum, O Tannenbaum
Grandma rocks to that tune
I hear it and see a corn-cob burning
cookstove on spindle legs in her kitchen
Grandma at a card table
playing canasta with Aunt Eleza
I thought Eleza Grandma's age
learned later she was a daughter-in-law
had married Herman
Grandma's eldest who died young
The two grew old together
playing canasta, rocking

O Tannenbaum, O Tannenbaum
Which one, which one, she'd say
are you? *Who's* are you?
Surrounded by so many grandchildren

she hardly knew us like
she knew Marlene, a distant cousin
who came in 1951 to Grandma's house
from an exotic place
East Germany
A pink-cheeked
reminder of the *old country*
she spoke of danger
in Grandma's native tongue
of her brother there, needing help
I stood near the rocker
not breathing, listening
not understanding a word

Grandma, tired of birthing babies
by the time my mom arrived
did not hand down her language
so I know the tune, but not the words
Did Grandma even know *Mom*
her last, eleventh child, ambitious
bossy, unhandy in the kitchen
How the brothers called her *captain*
how Brother Otto spanked
her, age seven, three times
for refusing (*Now I'll never ever do it*)
to pull cabbage stumps
with the others in the garden

O Tannenbaum, O Tannenbaum
Each summer after my visit
the tune of the old German carol
accompanying the Buntrock story
follows me south out of Columbia
past the park of reunions

the baseball diamond where my dad
played, dreaming of the majors
where I played my last real
ballgame at a Buntrock reunion
and, a different time, both grown
my brother and I together
ran a 3-legged gunny-sack race

The melody easily skips over
the Jim River, the dry summers
It follows me east toward winter
My own children outgrowing
their small town

CUT

I love original earth
like the pasture at home in Dakota
that's never been plowed
Its curves reveal the circular
shadows of Indian encampments
and pasque flowers' faint feathery blue
with saffron stamens reaching like feelers
I remember my mustang's hooves crushing them
yet the pasques return spring after spring
push up baked clay while tied to the earth's apron
Each year since then the land's curves
harbor pheasant-nest secrets
the broken shells of my memory
of mowing the blowing grasses, how
in the last round I'd leap off the tractor
to run through the narrow swath
of still-standing brome
to chase out the small furred and feathered
before finally thrusting the sickle through
Dad wondered what always took me so long
on that last round
and I never told him... I wish I had
But I had not yet learned what we had in common
the prairie in our veins like blood
Maybe if we'd each sliced a wrist
and held them tightly to each other
both of us would have been more grounded
Maybe everything else
would have been different

THE HEART OF THE MATTER

This house
raised against all odds
on the east side
of Sand Lake
in South Dakota, 1908
rebuilt itself
in my heart

In the years after
I was twenty
I moved fast, moved
eight different places
in fewer years
unaware that builders
had been contracted
were already at work
on a monumental
task in my heart's space...
oak bannisters and all

Seventeen
individually-carved
dowels to the landing
twenty-seven more
to the second floor...
The bottom pillar
with a loose lid
where kids
dropped a German
oak nutcracker
one holiday
We didn't tell--

he lay there years
Later I searched for him
with a flashlight
but he had gone
I do not know
his rescuer

No other truly
grand houses line
Sand Lake, the kind
with carved lintels
above each
downstairs window
and sliding oak doors
between the two
largest rooms

But even such a house
could not save
Grandma Herseth
from herself -- her
own dark interior
as Grandpa's large
laugh resounded
through its rooms
after he'd bet on horses
or drunk himself into stupor
in distant towns

This house's
attic in my heart
allows such a view

of distance
that to this day
hills or too many
tall trees closet me

Each spring
the pull on my body
home
foreshadows
the day my heart
falls down --
the great grandfather
clock finally quiet
in the heart's
room

A refinished bookcase-cum-desk
held cattle medicine
in my young Dad-helping days
The dining room still contains
the carved table, buffet
& eight chairs
my mother bought
for seventy-four eighty-eight
when she was very young
before her marriage even

My luck --
to be brought
to this house in 1940
a newborn, I know
its intimacies, every
depth of corner
I can move

in-its-dark-without-sound
my hand finding
light switches or landing places
before my head do⌐s

The women who come
to this house to live
with the men who own it
do not know their way here
as my sister & I do
and we banished ones
resent those
who later offer
civilly
to please feel at home

All the rest of the years
that they live
in this house
they will never carry
its great weight
in such a small place
as a heart

HOME PLACE

The shore of a sandy lake
abuts the edge of my memory
close
like the much-loved land

Some of us
mostly daughters
move away
but the feel
of earth between our toes
sun hot above grain spun to gold
chaff--an itch beneath our shirts
sweat, and the brief cool reprieve
of a reluctant rain
washing through the cracks
of western window frames
on the old home place
remain

vivid
as if being young there
had just happened
and our mother seated
in the shade of an elm shelling peas
lifts her head
at our father's call
from his pick-up truck window to come
check cattle at the Daker Place

The shore of a sandy lake
weaves along the reed-slim
edge of my memory

like the haunting land
Each autumn
I hear calves bawling
and the calling geese
blues and snows
fall from grace
in that season
Years gather like fleet
clouds on the horizon

GAME REFUGE

The South Dakota sky is immense
unbroken to the world's edge
Wind lashes water-reeds against the blue
In the distance herds of deer
bound above barley beards
like Swedish puppet reindeer
leaping off their strings
Nearby   a quiet heron on a long thin leg

A burst of rust spills onto the road
before my pickup-truck --
a small fox laced into the one-rut trail
Her tongue drips sweat for miles
before she glimpses space
and leaps   for wilderness

Imprinted by this place
I always forget to remember fall --
the constant season
of guns and men
and acrid ammunition scent

Forget to remember the hunting pits
lying deep in stubble corn
paneled even, hung with girlie pictures
In lovers' postures, guns
and men lie fused by blood
sweat   anticipation

in wait for me
For like the fox I'm in a rut   frantic
for that saving space
in which to dive   disappear
for an hour   a day
knowing never again   can it be for a lifetime
Not even one whole season

BARBED FENCES

Always there are fences
fencelines and fields of grain within
corn, oats, wheat, rye
Seldom flax, but when
there's flax behind a fence
the whole world comes blue
as though I lived
on a seacoast somewhere

Our fences ended at a lake
which kept our ranch
from falling off the spinning planet
Without that lake there
Grandpa would have just
kept on reeling land in

Only deer and trains
cross against the fencelines
I raced a train once
Dawdled on my horse
between a barbed-wire fence
and the railroad tracks
The steel one rose up suddenly
beside me, spooked my horse
and raced us toward the horizon

Each time I'm home
I take the pickup truck
and skirt the lake just
to look back down fencelines
In summer I can sight
down them like a surveyor

straight into the old days
And in any blizzarding winter
I can follow one, even barbed-wire
Seldom notice the ones
still keeping me in

HORSE

From 24 December to January 24
each day hangs opaquely toward earth
A horse from the past
            steps out of a foggy landscape
                    as I drive to the Cities
                            calling on the memory of horse:

                    Bessie, Gray Lady, Danderee
            the black one I never named
I remember the spirited sound, the hooves
            the ice-trip on this road to the airport at my father's dying
                    the dark snaking hearse-led line
                                    of cars through snow

                            The creature horse
            in my head   our source and connected
skin, a deep memory
            language resonating   from the withers

                            That black horse
            carrier of more than spirit but nothing
less, lived briefly on the land of my youth
                    my brother found it dead in a corn-stubble
field
            kept from food by the others
                            Fifteen years after
                                    I know it   as a sign

Horse-power, round of belly, great
in shoulder; aging, I come to look   like horse;   it has little to do
with a fast way out
Already I have lived
long at the edge   neither in nor out of town
My piece of grass too small for horse
or self

Once many horses, Angus too
ran in my father's fields, I thought
my inheritance contained them
then I married   traveled   birthed babies
learned
I left more
than horse behind

A pinto appears on the skyline
its black white arrangement
of skin moves close to the freeway; I leave the car   it will not
come   won't put its nostrils
remembered breath   into my palm

But someday the lost, unnamed one
will reappear   and prophesy   Till then I search
the winter prairie
roadways   and far pastures

SILOS

I was eleven, bored
and herding Dad's cattle
I was off the horse
Knew I was in the safest spot
in all the land
surrounded
by acres of grass
My horse and I
the tallest shadows anywhere
Soon I noticed
some short grasstips
mounded up nearby
A tiny hut, it seemed
with a hole in it
I sat down to muss it up a bit
Stuck my horse's
bridle rein deep inside
And three bared-teeth mice
came bristling out
They glared at me, then jumped
Again, again they jumped at me
and I moved swiftly back
Those little dagger teeth shone very white
and I a real danger felt
Only eleven
I didn't know
about the buried silos
in the prairie underbelly
About the reincarnation
of their guards

I know it well, it formed
a dam, held back the shallow lake
that would have drowned our farm
Grandpa forced its rise off South Dakota soil
with an old steam tractor, wheels wide
and heavy enough to make
a road just by rolling

It still runs strongly north and south
then trails east before it angles north again
to split our farmhouse off
from the barns, the cattle yards, and bins
No ditch on either side
till spring when the lake can rise
and seep in like years to line its tracks
Late in life my eyes veer west
toward the shimmering mirage of water
I see my young self
following grass-tufts
down the center of the road
In between the lines I'm
out of bounds, safe, like in a child's game
shared with errant badger's holes
laying claim to it like grandpa did
a couple of generations ago--
burrowed in for the long haul

Today from the road
I intently watch the horizon
for something looming
out of place: fox   deer
ruddy ducks   middle age
The road's still not been gravelled
it's barely even dirt
just two deep gashes
damming things up in my mind

TRIP HOME

Strange leave-taking time
We left in the morning dark
The white car sped west
over the seared prairie
The roots stretched down
as far as they could go
Mine too   No water
We stopped to drink
at a closed rest stop
drank the water brought along
for the radiator of the car
and swallowed the left-over miles
in gulps of sentences that
zoomed around inside like flies
bumping up against the windows
invading the rear windshield
as we streamed away

All the streams were dry
and I thought that the meeting we
headed toward would be for naught
a great zero in this
prairie pocket of drought
My mother would be there
You and I and my sister would be taken
for sisters several times that day
on the Aberdeen sidewalk
which steamed as you walked over it
in your red dress   a fuzzy-edged
desert mirage

The deserted unformed rows of corn
led home   their tassels gone
The pollen could not catch
the silken hairs growing out of ears

of absent corn   Even the small farm
where I'd rounded up yearlings
in a maze of wood corrals
had disappeared, crumpled
into a heap in my mind

I could not describe the absence
How the prairie'd taken a poison draught
I was swallowing hard trying
to tell you how it all had been
when I was eight   and we
collected testicles in buckets
near those absent barns
and took them home to supper
This visit is the hardest cut
For through your slitted eyes I peer
at what is no longer here

A great Canadian goose on guard
watches us come the back way
through the refuge
He knew   before I did
about the poison rampant in the corn
In the pupils of your eyes
I glimpse again what is no longer
As I walk you up the stairs of my farm home
a smell is rising from the basement
of long-spilled memories of milk
from a separator in an honored space
before the time of pasteurizers
and the changed taste of milk upon our tongues
Now just the barn cats know
the old flavor   white streams
shot straight from a cow's teat
into their mouths as I used to do

for myself while I sat milking
I sit here writing
a white stream of absence
pooling between the lines
as my roots lie out and dying
in the sear heat of this deadly summer

In the night rains come
a vengeance of white lightning not seen
all summer and the thunder jars
me awake to realize you've left the bed
to do exercises for your back
on the thick rug   hoping
crickets will not leap
from underneath your shoes stashed
under the bed on my girlhood floor

Floored by all the absence
abed I lie awake in lightning
trying to lighten the load I travel with
knowing   this is not my place
though I claim it
Not my right though my birth marks it
like an ancient cemetery
where my heart has turned to stone
and my body can always lie to itself
beside this refuge

We arise early in the morning
descend past the ghosts on the creaking stairs
note the ache of the grandfather's clock
groaning in its oaken cabinet -
strange family tree   And leave
a hint of artesian coffee on our breaths
We leave for the east - an unnatural direction

THE LAY OF THE LAND

Eight stories up looking down
on nothing I know
my eyes follow the river
From this distance
I cannot see that it is dirty
sludge almost   slow
Also it is night
the city's lights twinkle
like predators' eyes
come to the river to drink
some falling back   or stretching
up invisible streets
digging their claws in
The lights blink on off on off on
I turn from the window
stare at this strange room
which must also wink
out at the river
if anyone were out there to notice
No one is   no one knows
where I am
having fled recently to Cairo
in search of a time and a place
to live intensely   in the moment
and not know the lay
of the land like I do in Dakota

FLYING

UPON THINKING ABOUT THE WORD *FEMINISM*

I rest my front teeth gently on my bottom lip
and start into a quiet hum, both lips together
When a half smile separates the hum
the word is born: feminism
and it is good   I name it Good

It tastes of sisters, camaraderie, knowing men as friends
It sports the new mint side of an Anthony coin
            no one's small change, but round, real
            found at last   the long lost widow's mite

Good, it does not usurp; but reveals epiphanies
awakens men with as gentle nudges as sisters give each other
            to centers of a different order   different rhythms
            I call it Good   like kisses dreamt

Good, it grinds down competition's hard-edged sound
into a cabochon   new kind of cameo that releases
women's faces from that pink and thankless quest for youth
            which claims the lines around their mouths
            for lack of smiling's sake

Young girls could learn to like each other   share
lollipops and boys, and teach the boys that all the words
            for ineffectual are not female   The boys would listen
            learn to know that it was good - this new created
                    order, this new meaning

In country homes and cities, a new self-image could emerge
would sustain two fragile egos in one shared space
            each in need of nurturing   share chores, and love
            They would not wish for sons when birthing daughters

The word is Good in its true self - what we have understood
is not   From that fallow ground we reap only wind
weeds of anger, hate men
          and teach our children what the word is   not
          Such meager chickweed will not sustain the masses

          Is not, is not -- therein hides the key
          We are what men are not   I call it good
          to grow in pride of what we're proudly not

Share the birthing of this pride   claim our newborn
far-from-ugly babe   midwife us   Name it Good
and we will parent generations of a different rhythm
          not mutually exclusive but of a different notion
          that may not allow much time to polish wing-tipped shoes
                    or pack someone else's bags
                                        for business trips

FLYING TO IOWA

*When I lie in bed thinking of those years
I remember* your legs
how they dropped from your torso
and lit running   in California especially
especially at night when
you draped one over my hip
The beauty of the moon on our bones
How delicate the love was sometimes
The smell of semen right after
sweetened especially for my tongue
I think of the night we thought
we would fly to Iowa for the nationals
We could have died in the fog
It was our wedding night
The pilot screaming to the control tower
My bridesmaids with their heads in their laps
A miracle   I said it would be all right
not making love then
Told you to look for the morning
the fog lifting from the airfield
The lights going out at the edges of the strip

*line from Linda Gregg, <u>Alma</u>, *Balancing*
                              Everything

SMOKE

I am smoke, with grey hair
a will-o'-the wisp
who lit in your life
with more will than I ever let on
We tell a story in our family
of how you pursued me —
how I declined time
and time again in that first year
But even then I was smoke
and you were the air I would live in
Who knows where the spirit came from
out of which woods or which field
over which water
Anyway, the wind picked up
fanned the flame and
now sometimes a prairie fire rages
But you, smart like those old pioneers
always emerge from the sod hut you built
to save us, long ago
in that very first year

> *line from Linda Hogan, The
> History of Fire, <u>Savings</u>

RUNNING TO YOU

Would I were running to you:
The high and smile and strength
you know on country roads
in company   eludes us now
The years stretch
taut from that June day
in Aberdeen
to three children
dogs, cats, the white mice later

Your body tan the year around
glints beaded sweat   I always look
recall your touch   my fingers
sliding on those muscles
hard from running country roads

You pass abandoned barns
and houses falling down
where ordinary lives were spent
Now just the splintered walls
recall   as sparrows
dart in and out an upstairs
bathroom window
Strings of hay   or barley beards
from last year's stubble   dangling
in their beaks

And in one yard an empty well
its broken windmill props
in need of mending
before the wind can spin me

Would I were running
to you   your eyes
mine   and new

SACRIFICE

This is the time of year
when the sun insists
that I present myself
before its face, unclothed
Demands this ritual event
in sacrificial
                    overtones

Small leaves spiral
from the walnut tree
as though some giant handmaid
tossed them at my feet
I step into the glare
                    of gold

Under the sugar maple's blush
I lose all shame
My fingers take on the smell of fall
the dank perfume of fermenting
orchard fruit, lush in disarray
I sink into a trance
in the sun's slow, licking
                    inspection

At length, I lie exhausted
in the softest tufted grass...
and it comes to pass
that the sun pours molten down
on my bent head, my out-
stretched arms, and on my breasts
briefly warm
          before the days of wool, of cold

STATUE

Once in my young years upon a time
there was a party
and I went dancing
the ring 'round rosy
one nude man falling down
My husband and I upon leaving
and looking for our coats
lost each other
Next I saw him on a stair
statue stopped in its tracks
A beautiful party guest
his black velvet pants tugging down
I found my coat
swung out the door
walked away at 30 zero degrees below
under a white knife-blade slivered moon
snow banks all around high swooping
I pulled my skin tighter to its fur
The freezing gnawed each wrist
I kept going
knowing I would die each while
he did not come for me

FABLE

Now it came to pass
that she was only three
a golden apple-eating child
Yet she could stamp   her feet
and claim an old authority

Daddy, daddy   tell me
who's the fairest in the land?
You are, he'd say   you are
Then be the handsome prince
and wake me, Daddy, wake me now
He'd smile and   with a kiss
he would
On a Victorian chaise
she'd lie straight out
purse her tiny lips
tight-shut her eyes
as he   on bended knee
would kiss her cheek
She'd wake in glee
and spit   a piece of apple out

Then   Mommy, mommy   dearest
you be the wicked queen
Please, please, you be the wicked queen
And she   unthinking
would don a grim and cruel face
and cry
Come, come and eat
my daughter dearest
Eat this large red apple
the likes of which you've never seen
Come eat my large red apple

The child would
and feign a weakness   stagger
toward the chaise and wail
Daddy, daddy, be the handsome prince
and save me   wake me, Daddy, please
Again the kiss
the likes of which she would
not feel again
for years

For it came to pass
that on a visit of the mother's mother
as she watched the ancient rite replayed
the hundredth time   she said
Daughter, daughter, you know not what you do
The wicked queen   indeed
Stop, daughter, stop this poison game
And   once upon a time
they finally did

NORTHWOODS SUMMER

Teenagers touch in secret
and walk the backroads singing

Little kids swim, ski, play cribbage
and drink cool-aid
as though summer will never end
Their laughter skips waves
like smooth, well-slung stones
and falls into the lake
with the easy splash of sunsets.

Teenagers touch furtively
and walk the backroads singing

Adults mend the docks with planks
bought on borrowed time
They try to close the cracks
they have fallen between
easily as two-year-olds

Teenagers touch, innocent
and walk the backroads singing

Birds clutter the feeder
finches, grosbeaks, a yellow-shafted flicker
They chatter like wives
and don't know
they too have slim identities
till the appropriate book is read
documenting their flight plans
mating behavior   and drinking habits

Teenagers touch silently
and walk the backroads singing

63

Inside the cabin
an anniversary vase of wild daisies
and Indian paintbrush on the table
marks time with petal drops so qui et
only the grandmother hears

    the teenagers touch in secret
    and hum down the backroads

THE DAY OF HEARTS

You rarely write poems
Once when you did though
we were in a cabin far
from home before a fire
with our eldest daughter
and friends; I had asked
that we write, all of us
to honor the day
When you finally
finished, you left the poem behind

Had you no courage
to show me the sad words?
Or maybe it was not what you intended
to write   I know what I wrote
that day was not

Back here again
before the fire
I am unseasonably cold for March
danger in it
as though an unthoughtful moment could result
in maiming   or death

I know of some women
who crossed the Antarctic
pulling their provisions on sleds, no dogs
today all are losing toes

On the east coast
you are caught
in the storm of the century
as houses fall on their faces from cliffs
into the sea
Airports have shut down
people will die

Tomorrow under my own power
I will drive back to our home
Unlock the door for which you have forgotten the key   wait
for runways to open
for planes to fly
for I want your heart
before me   ablaze
like this fire
but also   I want the words

THE SMELL OF SILENCE

Silence
No answers
on the wind
I walk the early morning
highway and smell the worms
for in the night it rained
and a million earthworms
wrenched their thick soft bodies
up from depths of dirt
to crawl across the land
and die before the tires of cars
or bake in sun
Their silver tracks still glisten
then stop abruptly in lumps of flesh
their silent protest smashed
like mine
I breathe in
their silent smell
Ask why such desperate surfacing
Such deliberate death?
Is this why doves still mourn
a summer dawn
Or why a distant
startled rooster pheasant squawks?
Somewhere   someone's
human bomb has dropped
no global flash
no stormy wind of fire
just the smell
of silence

NINE MILES LATER:
WATCHING THE TWIN CITIES MARATHON

Which one of you, as I stood
on the bridge near Lake Nokomis
talking alternately with a fresh-eyed woman
from Colorado and cheering you on
Which of you looked
me in the eye, said thanks for being here
and nine miles later died?
Centuries ago I'd take the blame
just for crying out, great
you're looking great, keep it up --
like some wild-haired witch
playing havoc along the autumn edge of a road

So many victories, I said later
to anyone who would listen
not yet knowing one had been the greatest
and happened at the tape
near the state capitol building
like on the plains of Greece at Marathon

What a morning
Even the wind stood still for your passing
and every birch around Nokomis
reflected bark like bones into a sheen of water
In the dawn of the day I leave
will someone beside a road call out
Great, you're doing great
would I believe?
Have birches begun somewhere
to hunch beside a lake, a river
to whiten, to lie in wait?

CHANGE

THE FAMILY HEART STONES

I wear four stones round my neck
all in the shape of hearts
The ivory cabochon
for you so heavy
if I strode into Lake Superior
I might drown
        never to surface
                or finish my life

PROMISE

Up some narrow stairs
in a California student space
my waters broke
Now many dams downstream
the drought has come
And you are gone
The roads are parched
as corduroy rows of corn
inch their small heights up in scorching sun
wave meagre plumes of silk
at tassels yearning for the absent pollen
It is nature's natural cycle I suspect
and folks will struggle through depleted
But time is on our side and cool
northern air will gather overhead
in honor of an always coming season
You and we will walk in sun again
lightning flashing only at the edges

TORRENT

I remember rain like this
when I was twenty-five
an all-day trip to Cambridge
Rebecca three
David searching for
his dissertation advisor
who, on a leave from Stanford
writing on E M Forester
had stumbled on some photos
then lost them, very rare
I remember waiting
in a car all day and the rain
coming down, coming down
Rebecca three and full of questions
as the two of us stared out the sheeting
windows
at the old streets, sidewalks, spires
Cambridge in the distance
I remember grey
the buildings, the sky, even the red
volkswagen convertible from the inside
I remember waiting
David gone a long, long time
Twilight came
When I think back he
might not have returned
What then would we have done?
Flown home? Were we there in '65
just because he was

I remember rain like this another time
a house along a road in Minnesota
its red frame windows; peeling paint
After four days of springtime rains
the lost septic tank underground

groaned, turned over
then emptied itself up into the house
Asthmatic, David fled to his office
in the dead of night
to merely live
I don't remember
rain like that much inbetween

In Cambridge Rebecca had to pee
we did not know where we were
so I held her small self
over the nearby curbstone gutter
by our car and watched her yellow urine
hurtle down a slanting road
blended with the rain
Back in Northfield the children
headed for the woods to pee
small toothbrushes, glasses
of water clutched tight in their fists

Before school one morning
I found Allison on the lip
of our southwest window-well
proud in her comfort
as she pooped in our yard

I don't remember how long
my hair was in either instance
or how I was as woman
wife, or mom, no journals live to tell
In the first siege of pouring rain
I was not a writer
In the second siege, ı was
I don't remember all
of how that came about
But this is some

Those long Midwestern winter days
children in and out of doors

in and out of snowsuits, forts, and boots
so many times a day
Always it seemed they had to pee
I would dress them down to skin
then dress them up again
In both instances I was
young, I didn't know it then

I know my father was alive
in the first rain, gone in the second
Like Beret's husband in *Giants*...
he disappeared in the dead of winter
I know that
the young woman holding
the girl above the gutter
on the Cambridge street
as pee streamed away to rain
knew very little really
about who she was in Cambridge
or why she had become the mother
of that child, or what the price
Nor had she learned much
ten years later though
her Dad had left
the family and his life
and she'd taken a job for a little money
then picked up a pencil and talked

I know David never found
his academic advisor
that day in Cambridge
when I was twenty-five
After hours of search
he returned to the car
We all went dolefully home
the windshield wipers slashing
That's all I ever saw of Cambridge in my life
And I know we found the septic system

After days of search and authorities
even a husband-wife team with witching rods
we found the poison gas
forced it back into the ground
The kids have grown now far too old
to hold over any gutter

I remember phone calls then
that magic feat of someone's
voice whom you love
flying over wires to yours
telling you something that changes you
right were you stand
like a godmother's wand
Like Mom's call that January
saying Dad had fallen dead
A big man, gone right to the floor
guest in a friend's kitchen
Mom snowbound at the ranch
cloistered in an upper bedroom
with their shared history
No one could reach her for hours
When the state snowplows
finally got through
she'd been glad
she could not be reached
Rebecca remembers
me taking that call
the look on my face, the crying
How the snow came down
ice too, a sheet of glass
carried us to the last airflight
out of Minneapolis for days

I don't remember how I felt
about that call as I remember
waiting in the volkswagen
on the grey Cambridge street years before

I don't remember taking the kids to Ruth's
but I remember deciding to
I don't remember the details
of my mother's long night of talking
about her Buntrock family
when we arrived for the funeral
but I remember she told us
told us and told us
She could not stop telling us
not of Dad's life but of hers

I wish to inform myself
about that young woman lost in Cambridge
with her child splay-legged over a gutter
I would like to talk
with the somewhat older
young mom of three, who sent them
into the forest, not with crumbs
but toothbrushes and water instead
as the rains came

I want rain to pour when it is needed
like tears; but to stay in the heavens
when corn is already as tall as the sky
I want rain for cleanness
not for drowning
Rain to make distance easier on eyes
with little pigment in them
but not for endless days of flood
I want a bridge
from the volkswagen in Cambridge
over the child, the death
the reluctant septic system
the woman who could not be reached
the other one who cannot remember
Over the torrent
transforming ever since

LAKE SUPERIOR GEODE

Four Catholic sisters
sun on a granite settle
Two loons, dressed similarly
float in the background
Much sun falls onto my back

Covered with hot flashes
I am my own magnetic field
Storms can arise in me
that may affect
large sections of the land

I remove my bandeau top
and press my breasts to the hot
Superior stone the better to hear
the shoreline's thump
The lake and I lie there
a long, long time
heart to heart
The loons mark it
I copy their laugh

Later along the shore
I find four ordinary stones
My daughter who loves stones
would pass them by
but they show me the way
to the sheer crystal underside
of a fifth stone where

I crawl in nursing the ache
caused by this age past fifty
crystalized
deep in my interior
Become my own geode
there's no mortal way out

HAND-ME-DOWN

I am fifty for three days now
and today comes a letter
in my mother's hand
She's remembering
and tells me of that remembering
How on the day that I was born
I was stubborn and
did not want to leave her
the warm pouch
How I did not yet care
about the outside wonders
She tells me how, inexperienced and
uninformed
she learned to push alone
and at ten p.m. on a Saturday in 1940
she gathered her whole blood from the source
and pushed me out into the light
so that today a half century later
I can read aloud a poem
from a daughter in Washington DC
and last night heard a song
coming down the centuries
on my other daughter's tongue
a seer, echoing her sister
Mama, I am coming home
Leaving taught me
how absurd it is to think
that we can ever leave
An oriental fan of cherry blossoms
arrives from my son in Japan
I think of him there
how he writes on the fan

he wants to hear my voice
I know what he means
because just last Sunday
I walked to church nearly singing aloud
because *my* mother and I had talked
an hour on the phone
of family things close to the bone
to hers, to mine, and flesh of her flesh
I was warm and walking, almost singing
my heart throbbing its regular beat
with the odd click I've been told
that sometimes mothers
hand down to daughters
I think to myself
I should remember to tell them
tell them it's perfectly natural
Tell them not to be alarmed
when they are told
of the click, the heart's wonder
that I too hand down...

DEATH CAN COME AS YOU SIT
IN A CAFE QUIETLY TALKING

It can lie on its side
blending in
and slip down your throat
with the ease of a pin
baked into French bread
when it falls
from the upstanding collar
of a busy shopkeeper up at five a.m.
rolling out dough on her sideboard
She hurriedly
fastens a blouse with it
where a button's dropped off
but refusing the task
it falls to the dough
toward a destiny
beyond itself
till it is lifted up
in clenched amazement
between the forefinger and thumb
of a chewing, visiting woman
who struck something firm
between her molars
hesitated, almost swallowed
kept talking and chewing the bread
with her friend in the cafe
She places the pin on a serving tray
like a scalpel and gravely
shows the proprietress
It lies there innocent
awaiting the next hand
that will put it to use

MOON PAUSE

These are the months of dark blood
and waiting. For the body
will move to a new state, uprooted
It will not be like moving
home, although the distance isn't far
but rather like marrying
into a close-knit private family
where all the bones are alien
to one's own, yet the passage is one.

OMEN

It was not good luck last night
to find a real chewed-on rabbit's foot
on the bedroom floor
but an omen
of this time in life for me

I picture the rabbit out there
somewhere, huddled beneath a bush
screaming silently
as rabbits can   Or   maybe   it's just hunks of fur
cast far abreast the carcass
camouflaged babies
somewhere   hiding in the grass

My birthright set of years
has half wound down   the childrens' choices
ones I would not choose
A spirit in the wind
bodes ill this spring
for near Alaskan shores
birds plunge in oil
leaking from an Exxon tanker

Feathers clog and part
the cold creeps in
Even arctic birds cannot survive the poison
licking at the flanks of land
My blood slows down
Arms and legs begin to feel it first:

the age-old glacial truth
that cannot take the heat   of years
but drips an unseen   melt of blood
in deep climactic change
Outside the dog   still waits
for me to toss the foot to her

BONES BECOME DUST

Bones become dust
yet skin drapes them
Friends notice, but
the real crumble's
invisible, like a mind
leaving a crime scene

NIGHT DROWNING

I wake
weak as a runt
kitten before milk
arms numb
from pinky finger
to elbow
No one
can tell me
what intrusion
this is
where it comes
from
at which hour
except night
Always
in the dark
I struggle back
to alive
mouth
shrunken
lips too large
for their opening
small trails
of wrinkles
purse
the aperture
A curse floats up
through dimensions of water
toward dawn

BONE SPIRIT

A ghost rises from this body
about 2:30 a.m., and leaves
Thirst tears the insides
of my cheeks, tears at the fattened tongue
The body-shell cannot
get out of bed, even for water

Bones hollow in the night
teeth sit loosely in their holes
lining a jaw that cannot clamp
The ghost that has bided
its time for 50 years
has found an opening
an exit   an out

All day the day before
the body had rocked back on its heels
then forward to the numb balls of its feet
The spirit in the bone of each step
knew something was up, prepared
as it was for leaving

That night when the body indeterminate
startled to wakefulness
it barely discerned a shadow
slipping out into the cold
through a nearby window

                    however, the family dog, awake
& aging   attempted a warning
          for its spirit recognized one
                    of its own coming clear in the room
                         It heaved congestive breath
          toward its heart tearing at the cage

          and from 3 a.m. through all
the next day   sucked at its own throat
          lungs sweating blood, unable to tell
                    how it now dreaded the on-coming night
                         the inner one coming alive

This body
changed
before my eyes
and I was
helpless
to stop it

Young I
had thought
I was in charge
could will myself
tall, slim
almost happy

But the body
had other
ideas
lowered its center
of gravity
from the head
to the belly
preparing
for   *I don't*
know what

although the bones
talk among
themselves, mostly
at night
and I dream
in their language
Come morning
I cannot recall
dialect, inflection
especially
meaning

TOO SOON SEPTEMBER

A strong wind rattles
these pages in my hands
like someday my bones will
as my breath leaves
Two hundred miles south
my husband works on a wedding
Two thousand miles to the east
our daughter prepares
I try to mark it
About the diligent man, her father
About the young woman
who thinks a lot like me
except passionately
Where did such passion come from?
Or rather, where did mine go?
Turning fifty took so much out of me
In one flash, bones weakened
and skin whitened
like so much parchment
My legs have become stiff as birches
Suddenly, surrounded by seagulls
I thrust my neck up, back, up again
and am walking and screaming
In angry preening, I walk and scream
My knees, like the gulls'
have grown knobby
and covered with years
My husband stretches his hand
north over the fir trees toward me
He means to pluck me back into this body
he loves, yet I know i am leaving
I wait for a wedding
that will spirit her away
yet I am the one who is going
My hope is, the ceremony
will distract everyone
Maybe even, no one will notice

END TIMES

I have come to rock again, the drop
of gulls a great whitewash of the past year

High in the atmosphere a jet trail breaks
cannot maintain a pattern either

the very air is stacked against it
Seagulls are aflap

I hear the nearby birches shiver
although the day is hot, for winter

is on the wind. A woman on the shore throws
scraps to squawking birds, they sink in waves

reflect the end of marriages, holidays
loaves of bread, and summers

Goodbye, Joyce, I hardly knew you
And did not know my brother till

he leaves you. Back at school his daughter
begins to learn of a certain shabbiness

that pulls at her wool jacket like beggars do
on the street corners of Washington, D.C.

She too wonders where summer's gone
The lady keeps throwing

her scraps to the wind as hungry gulls rise
out over the great water, screaming

Incessant waves push back from the land
as an August moon comes on hard

pulls at them, at me, like you
did my breasts this long afternoon

Later a firefly flints off the moon, bursts
onto the deck, we read in its light

till morning arrives through the thin air
hugging the lake, the moon evaporates

Adrift on this island
I stretch my legs, one wing toward the lake

From the deck I am captured, a photograph
simultaneous click of the heart

The night we came there was a great storm
rocked the bed through lightning, thunder, but little wind

Electric eels wounded the sky in all directions
We finally slept

Between the 5th & 6th rib of your left side
a mark, a small moment of brown skin

a singe the size of my mother's slit
I escape a second time, sit by your side now

more than 30 years, did not fly
Days of sun bake my skin, brown it

stretch it out on the rock below our cabin
I will return disguised a year from now

speaking a foreign language
Voices arc down the path under leaning bushes

Strangers step onto *our* deck
I cannot welcome them; alone on my slant of stone

I stretch my breasts toward the late sun
as the pale moon slips out of the way

One seagull homes in
At the last minute veers south

completes a low full circle
one wing tapping the water, biding time

All my life I will know this stone, a pallet
where my fleshy back fits, a haunch

where my head can rest gratefully
Still, skin prickles in the late sun

A mountainous woman comes up from the water
takes up the whole path leaving, the great lake recedes in her
wake

The gull people take over the rocks
all sizes, demeanors

most a mottled, indiscriminate color
But one white sentinel gull claims the most jutting rock

keeps an eye on me, settles in to wait
The others sweep out over the water

till aground again, they pick at themselves, sharp beaks
searching, scraping, weird knees bent forward

Some face off, glare, scream at each other
A few doze, bury their heads in feathers amid such crying

I lie there, watch one particular gull
eyeball to eyeball over a slope of stone

Skull to skull together we are small rocks in the shape of bones
I name the place golgotha, get up and go home

SNAP

All my bones snap
at each other
remembering the forced feeding
of estrogen; made of mare's urine
not what it's touted to be
poisonous, even

JOURNEY

It was time to get on
Unthinking, we went through the door
found seats, settled in
The motion moved us, was good
Time passed
We made small choices --
to read, nap, or visit
The inexorable swept us toward
a future moment we could not choose
nor would it wait
like music we know will end
played on a violin
by a pregnant friend
immensely present for the occasion
The future moves toward us all
We ask to get off somewhere convenient
But no one hears
It will stop when it will
even if by accident
I rise to get a drink of water
Small wrecks can be seen out the window
The embankments are very steep